A GORiLLA RiDiN' ON
A HALF A HOT DOG

JACLSON,
          PLEASE STAY COOL! I HOPE
yoU ENJOY MY BOOK

A GORILLA RiDiN' ON A HALF A HOT DOG

H Rick Goff

To order additional copies of this book, contact:
Xlibris
1-888-795-4274
www.Xlibris.com
Orders@Xlibris.com
710416

CONTENTS

This book is dedicated to my wife Carol, my two knuckleheads, Justin and Austin (not twins) and to all fathers of boys!

Raising kids, boys in particular, in the world we live in today is a daunting task that requires very unique skills. Well maybe not so much skill but at the very least, patience and a willingness to stay in the batters box with a 90-plus fastball aimed directly at your head. With all of the distractions that our young men face, we as Fathers, have to make sure that we are heard above all the other chatter i.e. video games, phone calls, loud music, text, tweets etc! We have to talk louder (yell in some cases) to make sure that we are not only heard but clearly understood—I'm not sure this is really possible with boys—hard to think they can actually hear you and understand you at the same time! We have to make sure that we understand that the psychological makeup of boys prevents them from grasping a concept as complicated as paying attention and actually doing what they are told and most importantly when they are told to do it! I really shouldn't try to get too analytical here because I am not a degreed child psychologist; the only qualification I possess is that I AM A FATHER—the Father of two boys who are now Men. The Father of two knuckleheads who over the years have made me laugh and cry (sometimes both at the same time), but most importantly they have made and help me understand what and who I truly am.

The title was inspired by my oldest son Justin. It's a simple story that is powerful in its simplicity. As a young child I can remember looking up and without giving it much thought, see that a cloud formation resembled something familiar. I can recall seeing the faces of various things from people to animals in cloud formations. I have seen the most common things like Abraham Lincoln's face, a lion and even my fifth grade teacher Mrs. Boyd (she was one of my favorite teachers of all time). My point here is that I can only recall seeing things that were somewhat familiar to me. I taught (well we did it a lot) my boys the art of cloud watching at an early age and it's something that we always enjoyed (I still do today). Once while cloud watching in the backyard with my boys, who were 8 and 3 at the time, Justin looked up and boldly proclaimed "Look Dad, I see King Kong ridin on a half a hot dog! I looked up and after a few seconds I could clearly see the outline of King Kong (giant gorilla) on half of a hot dog bun—sure enough I too saw King Kong Ridin on a Half a Hot Dog! Most times a formation would only last a few seconds, but this one seemed to linger. Even little Austin saw King Kong on that half a hot dog. We laughed and I thought to myself—what great imaginations these boys have—they make me proud to be a Father.

Note—My Boys/Men make me proud every day! Justin is now 27, a college graduate and out in the world finding his own way. Austin is now 21 and a college senior. They are both fortunately fine young men who seem well adjusted and on their way to becoming productive members of society; but when I look at them I hope they both continue to see "King Kong Ridin' On a Half A Hot Dog"

BOY PHRASES

You know you're the father of two boys when you hear the following phrases:

I did all of it......except! (Well you didn't do it all!!)
I never touched it!
I didn't do it!
Whaaat!!
I thought it was mine!
Mommy said I could!
Daddy said I could!
When is Mommy coming home!
It's not my turn to take out the trash!
I washed my hands!
I took a bath yesterday!
I did it last time!
I closed that door!
It just stopped working!
It was working last time I used it!
The towel just caught on fire! (AFTER IT WAS PLACED IN THE OVEN)
The pajamas were smoking so I took them outside and laid them on the driveway!
It was just a fender-bender!
The mailbox came out of nowhere!
It just broke!
I don't know how that sock got in the motor of the ceiling fan!
I just borrowed it!

He didn't ask!
Big brothers don't have to ask!
I did the homework but forgot to turn it in!
I love my little brother!
I miss my big brother!
Can I get Justin's room when he leaves?

PANCAKES

I once recall watching Justin sitting on the stairs (he was 3 years old), his elbows on his knees and the palms of his hands on his cheeks, his eyes straight ahead but blank because I sensed he was in the deepest of thought. My chest poked out as I watched my little genius racking his brain trying to figure out some great mystery of our time. Just how did those Egyptians build those pyramids? How can we get a manned spacecraft to Mars? What other energy sources can we harness? Well being a new father I felt it appropriate to enter the domain of a little boy and try and see what great problem of life had put his young wheels in motion. I felt like he might reveal some hidden secret that may possibly expand MY horizons. I carefully took a seat next to Justin on the stairs and since I didn't want to break his concentration—I gently asked him while almost whispering, "What cha thinking bout

Sport". Without moving his hands from his cheeks or changing his glance he simply said, "pancakes". Yep—PANCAKES! I asked him, "Well, what about pancakes?" He said again without changing his expression, "Eatin' pancakes." My little Einstein was thinking about eating pancakes, not how to make better pancakes or the ingredients for pancakes but simply "eating pancakes". An experienced father probably would have ignored his first born son sitting on the stairs in what appeared to be deep thought and went on to the den to read the paper, but first-time fathers will fall for it every time. They will be struck by the notion that they may have been involved in creating the next great thinker i.e. Aristotle, or the next great scientist like Einstein or even the next great President like Lincoln, when actually all he has really done is help create a little boy who likes to eat pancakes.

WHEN DO I GET MY WiFE BACK?

There never has been, nor will there ever be, anything quite so special as the love between a mother and a son.—Author Unknown

Having kids was one of if not the highlight of our marriage. Carol and I always wanted kids and we both agreed that we wanted boys. We were always excited about the fun we would have with six little knucklehead boys (ok the six idea was mine—the pump was shut off at two little knuckleheads) running around the house, doing their chores, helping Mom with their siblings, never fighting! It was going to be great—I could have my own basketball team or field over half of a baseball team. We named Justin years before he was born. We once told Carol's mother we were going to name our first son Justin Case and she disapprovingly asked why Justin Case? I should have let Carol answer this one, but he of the quick wit quickly chimed in "Just-In Case he's not mine" as my mother-in-law's Medusa-like stare slowly turned me into stone, I quickly realized that I had not gained any son-in-law points. My weak attempt at humor confirmed all of the reservations she had about her daughter marrying me in the first place—I think this is where the die was cast for my years of agony. Anyway I survived this one and Carol and I went on to produce Justin Rickey (and yes he is mine).

As new parents we were quite thrilled with our handiwork—he was absolutely the most beautiful baby ever. He slept all night, changed his own diapers, got up to get his own bottle in the middle of the night, never cried and Daddy was his first word—of course most of this is not true. He was a fairly typical little bundle of joy—he didn't sleep all night and he cried some, and of course he didn't change his own diapers or get up to get his own bottle in the middle of the night, but DaDa was his first word! However, I noticed early on that he was not into sharing his mother with me. She was his and that was the end of that. I remember pulling him aside once and giving him the rules of the house—what I call the Mommy/Wife rules. He was probably a year old (not too young to let him know that his mommy was also my wife). "Look Buster," I said—she was mine before she was yours—you can have her from morning until early evening, but the rest of the time she is mine— get it". This in essence left me with maybe 3 (probably more like 2.5) hours—Carol was out like a light by 9:30 most of the time. Justin seemed to understand the rules at the time, but his actions later proved otherwise. "Read me another bedtime story" (they would both fall asleep) bad dreams, thirst, etc became the norm— mommy time was far outweighing wife time. I tried once again when he was a little older to give him the Mommy/Wife rules— he was 3 and I really thought he should have gotten it by then. Again he listened intently and afterwards seemed to understand that Mommy had to be shared with Daddy. By the way, Mommy seemed content to let the boys fight it out—I think she enjoyed the attention and the big fuss made over her. Justin eventually understood the Mommy/Wife rules and reluctantly backed off a bit when he was around 5, but that was just when Austin came along. As a logical dad, I logically assumed that Justin would explain the Mommy/Wife rules to Austin. No such luck, Austin was even worse; he wanted Mommy all the time and had no intentions of sharing her with either of us. Once again Mommy let the boys fight it out, she couldn't lose—it was a win win for her (now I know why she didn't want to have girls—she didn't want the competition). Justin and I both eventually had to get Austin in line and teach him how to share Mommy. Now again, I assumed as they became teenagers that the Mommy/Wife rules were well established and they very well knew and understood the boundaries—this too like many of my assumptions with my boys, proved to be a bad one. They both still had and have memory lapses (something boys never outgrow) and have to be reminded of the rules. I really don't know the answer to the original question "When do I get my wife back?' Mommy still just lets the boys fight it out!

IT COULD HAPPEN

I think little boys function on a totally different plane than the rest of us. What they conceive they definitely try to achieve. Computers, computer games, the Internet, airplanes (jets), race cars, monster movies, and the Web had to come from the mind of a little boy thinking "wouldn't it be neat if this could do that". I looked at my boys sometimes and just wondered how fast the rat in the wheel could really run. You just never know what they will come up with next. So you just go with the flow and let their creative minds work. Who else could have invented an engine but a little boy—who else could have thought they could fly but a little boy. I didn't strap on wings as a young boy to try and fly but I did try to float off the top of the house with my mother's umbrella once (Mary Poppins style)—broke the umbrella and my arm! However I do recall flying (maybe floating) for just a second!!

We were flying kites one day off of a rather steep cliff near our home. The wind off the cliff really gave the kite tremendous lift and it literally almost became a dot in the sky. We would tie at least three 300 ft kite strings together so that the kite would just go higher and higher. "It's going into space" said a wide eyed Austin (who was 3 at the time) during one of our kite flying outings. I almost went into a long adult type explanation as to why the kite couldn't literally go into space. Something like, "Well before it goes into space it must enter and make it through the earth's lower atmosphere and even before then the kite is so light that it may get caught in the jet stream and literally be torn apart......! Fortunately the thoughts never made it from my brain to my mouth and I simply said—"yea if we tie another spool of kite string to it the kite might just make it into space". Justin who was 8 and pretty smart (at the time) knew that no matter how many spools of kite string we tied together the kite would never go into space, but he gave his little brother a reassuring look and pat on the head saying "It could happen."

"I DIDN'T DO IT"

While the phrase "I didn't do it" is probably common in any home with kids, it takes on a totally different meaning with more than one boy in the house. Boys have a way of "doing it" even when they really didn't do it. They can do things that defy all logic and in most cases all the laws of physics—just how can a sock get lodged in the motor of a ceiling fan?? Austin had a way of making the impossible a reality and could explain it away with a convincing "I didn't do it." You know what? Most of the time, I really don't believe he knew he did it—thus maybe he really didn't do it even if he did it--better stop this—it makes my hair hurt. Anyway he had no recollection of how he did these things—they literally just happened around him. He didn't know how the sock got in the ceiling fan—he was probably just twirling it around and the next thing he knew it was gone! Just like that, it was not in his hand anymore and he was just twirling air. Was he curious as to why the sock was gone? Did he wonder where it had gone? No, he just simply moved on to something else like, taking the old radio apart. The sock was gone and that was the end of that. A month later when the ceiling fan wasn't working and the handy man—a guy I called to look into things like this since my home repair ended at changing light bulbs and air filters—opens up the guts of the fan and finds the blue sock we had been looking for every Sunday morning before Church for the last four weeks. He looks perplexed and somewhat stupefied, but I look at him and say plainly "You obviously don't have kids and if you do, they are definitely not boys." We never did figure out how that sock got inside the ceiling fan and Austin stands by his original claim "I didn't do it."

"IT WAS JUST A FENDER BENDER"

16-year-old drivers are the scourge of our society. A 16-year-old behind the wheel of a two-ton vehicle, well maybe just one ton since they are all made of fiberglass these days, can cause more mental anguish than watching a teen movie—any teen movie, take your pick. My son was trained by the best of the best of drivers— he received well over 100 hours (my wife would say 30 minutes) of top notch instruction from a master driver—a driver who had driven all over the world from the winding roads of Bavaria to the parking lots called the LA Freeway system. He could not have received better training if we had paid for it—the instructor of course was ME! The proud father who was ready and willing to share his knowledge and mastery of the highway with his first born son was yours truly, yes naïve me! I remember the day I basically issued a self-fulfilling prophecy by telling everyone in my office that I was turning my son loose on the streets in a big metal machine (again maybe more fiberglass) that I am sure he had fully mastered under my expert tutelage—he was ready to drive and I knew he was prepared because I prepared him.

It happened while I was on a business trip—I got the call from my wife that started with "Justin is alright" all this meant to me was that he wasn't killed so I get to kill him. She went on to say that the car "my car" was not alright. My car was now what the insurance company calls "totaled." Well Carol started to give the details, "he was going around a curve and this mailbox came out of nowhere" and she suddenly stopped mid-sentence with a frustrated "why don't I just let Justin tell you what happened". I should have declined this offer since I pretty much knew his explanation wouldn't pass anybody's logic test, let alone mine. But Carol was quick to give him the phone and in the split second I had between him getting on the phone and starting to speak, I tried to brace myself for what I knew was going to be some lame brained teenage excuse about the mailbox suddenly appearing out of nowhere and I couldn't avoid it, but it was too late, he was already speaking and before I could get my guard up, it came out of his mouth "It was just a fender bender." In his mind a completely smashed front end and destroyed dash board (the air bags went off) was "just a fender bender." It was too funny for me to be mad at him—I wanted to ask him if he really knew what a fender was or at least the difference between a fender and a dash board but at this point I decided why bother. I concluded that even though the car was totaled, at the end of the day Justin was alright and it really was "just a fender bender."

WHO KNEW?

Boys have many hidden talents that always present themselves at the most inopportune times. I never knew Justin could burp so loud until once we were having a dinner party with friends—Buuuuuuuurrrrrrrrrrrp—I thought it would never end. He actually seemed rather proud of his new found talent and he matter-of-factly responded to his achievement with a simple "Everybody burps." I guess he was technically right. You never really know when boys are ready to be presented to the rest of society so you just play it by ear and take your chances. Loud burping, purple nurbles, wedgies, and nuggies are just a few of the unsung talents of boys. Where do they get these things??? Is it in the "How to be a Boy" book that only they know about or is it all natural i.e. it's just their nature? I don't know for sure and will not venture into this technical territory to try and explain the unexplainable. Boys will be boys!! Every so often though they will throw a hard curve ball right at your head, just as you are about to duck and take cover, it breaks right down over the plate for a strike. Justin did this to me once when he decided he wanted to play the bass guitar for a band—Carol and I are musically challenged and had no inclination that either of our boys would be interested in music. During middle school, Justin met Alex, Chris and Nathanial and they wanted to start a band—Alex and Chris played decent lead guitar (for 7th graders) and Nathanial played drums. So they wanted Justin to be the bass guitar player. Never mind that he didn't even know the difference between a bass guitar or any other type of guitar, never mind that he hadn't played any instrument since the Playskool xylophone he banged on as an infant. This is how the minds of boys work—remember, if they can conceive it, making it a reality is in the bag. Alex, Chris, Justin and Nathanial were starting a band and needed a bass player and Justin was it! Not a thought was given to the fact that he didn't know how to play bass guitar and more importantly, he *didn't have* a bass guitar. Justin came home one day and proudly told us he was in a band. What type of band I asked; he said a rock band (we later discovered much to our chagrin that it was a punk rock band) and asked if he could have a bass guitar. I almost laughed out loud but I sensed he was serious so I figured I had better at least look serious and hear him out. He told me the story about the boys in the band and I patiently listened. I finally felt it was time to remind him that he didn't know how to play the bass and had not shown any interest in music—ever. I asked Justin, well who is going to teach you to play bass guitar—he proudly said, Alex. Well he was convinced that he was a bass player without knowingly ever seeing a bass guitar. I finally bowed to the pressure--Mom was on his side and I really didn't stand a chance anyway.

We went out and bought a bass guitar for Justin and I waited for it to be tossed in the closet and start gathering dust like the Teenage Mutant Ninja Turtle bus and the Battle Bots he also had to have. Well to my great surprise, in about two weeks he came home from "band practice" and he could actually play the bass guitar—I don't mean just thumbing the strings, but he could actually carry a beat. I was surprised that I was surprised—I should have known that boys can do whatever they really set their minds to do. Now I was quickly brought back to earth when I realized the band called Pushover was a punk rock band that played loud music with unrecognizable lyrics—I figured out that every song sounded the same so I guess it was easy for Justin to learn how to play the same notes. However, the band did go on to cut a CD (maybe two—I went deaf after the first one), play at local parties and clubs over the next three years. I think the CDs are still available and you should try and pick one up—it's really not bad for a group of 7th graders. Who knew?

HOMEWORK

Do you have any homework?? Uuhhh I think so! Why don't you know if you have homework or not? Did the teacher not tell you?? Did you not think to write it down? "No, I thought I could remember it" Now for someone who can't remember to brush his teeth in the morning do you really think you could remember your homework? This is a conversation that I have had with both my boys since they entered academia. This homework thing is something we just never mastered. The homework hotline, homework time i.e. no TV or video games until you finish your homework, homework pencils, even a string around the finger—you name it, we tried it, but homework was (is) always an issue. "Don't you want to go to college to expand your mind?" (Literal translation—you need to plan on leaving my house) Well, you'll never get to college if you don't remember to do and turn in your homework. Yes that was an issue too—I sort of assumed (another bad assumption) that if you get pass the getting it done part you were in there, but nooo my friend, our homework sometimes never made it out of the book bag into the teachers homework bind. "I know you did it" "I saw it" "I even helped you with it!" How can you do your homework and forget to turn it in? (This answer could probably be in the I Don't Know section) To this point I am thinking that schools and teachers should rethink the homework deal—I would be willing to let them stay in school longer if they would not put me through the torture and stress of making sure homework is done—most of it I can't do anyway and I have an advanced degree. Homework would ruin my mood when I came home and either got a report that it wasn't done, turned in or I actually had to help do the homework. Were you not paying attention in class? Didn't the teacher show you how to do the assignment? Did you look in the back of the book? (always worked for me). Well somehow the homework would eventually get done but I would still long for the day when there would be no homework—it's too tough on a Dad!

"SPORTS ARE JUST NOT ME"

We had just finished one of Justin's soccer matches and were riding home and Austin who was still in a car seat looked at me through the rear view mirror and out of nowhere goes "Dad, sports are just not me." I tried not to react to his comments since after all he was barely four years old and couldn't yet know who he was, let alone know that sports are not for him. But he kept looking at me like he wanted to discuss this issue immediately and get it off his chest—almost like he wanted me to pull the car over and have the debate right then. Now I am a big sports fan and always enjoyed participating and watching the big three (football, baseball and basketball—and now that I'm over forty—Golf is on the list) Remember I had visions of fielding my own team of Goff boys before Carol shut the factory down. I gave up on the team but was hoping for a couple of jocks who could carry their weight. Well Austin was not having anything to do with this sports thing—participating or watching. I always knew Austin and Justin were quite different in their makeup; Justin was outgoing, personable and needed to have friends around him all the time. However, Austin even as an infant was very content with playing by himself—I would always say, he didn't need the rest of us and he just tolerated us since we were around anyway. Here he was barely potty trained proclaiming that sports were not for him and challenging me to make sure I understood the deal. Well he promptly forgot about it as soon as a butterfly flew pass the window but guess what—he never has had any interest in sports unless you consider "Track and Field" a major sport (maybe in Europe)—I only really watch or care about track every four years when the Summer Olympics roll around. Austin did come home one day during his freshmen year in high school and simply said "I'm running track and need some running shoes." Actually he was participating in the hammer toss! I guess sports were just not him!

"I JUST FiGURED IT OUT"

While I did say earlier that Carol and I were musically challenged—she is a bit more challenged than I am (risky to say but I think she would agree). I did play the bass violin in my high school orchestra—never mind that I thought and still think a C note is a hundred dollar bill, but once someone tuned it for me, I could read the music and sometimes make a joyful noise. I will never forget the concert that we played Fiddler on the Roof (I know I 'm really dating myself)—I still hum those tones (Matchmaker, If I were a Rich Man) today. However, baseball was more of my passion and making the baseball team meant the bass violin was out of the picture. But it seemed I did carry a couple of musical genes, I had always wanted to learn to play the piano and when I turned 40 I made it a goal to make this happen. I went out and bought a keyboard with high hopes of playing at Carnegie Hall within the year—well if not Carnegie Hall I could at least play in my den for my loving family. However somehow life got in the way again and the piano became another pipe dream. The keyboard was abandoned and collecting dust next to the tread mill when Austin apparently found it when he was around 8 and starting playing around with it. Now Austin was fiercely independent as a little boy and could do anything he set his mind to—I really don't think he ever even crawled--he went directly from laying in his crib to walking, not pulling up on the coffee table and taking baby steps but literally out of the crib and walking!!

Even with his independent streak, we were still surprised that the keyboard actually kept him occupied longer than his favorite cartoons and kid shows. He would tell us once we unknowing to him, heard him playing something and asked how he learned to play it, "I just figured it out." Well Carol seized on his apparent interest in the keyboard and immediately got him set up for lessons with a local piano teacher. In the back of my mind, I'm thinking this will last about two lessons and he will be hiding under the bed to keep from going to another piano lesson. It will be like going to visit the dentist and watching a movie Mom and Dad wanted to see! Fortunately, he didn't hide and I can't say he actually enjoyed the lessons, but he went (with only a few threats from Carol) and has now become an excellent piano player and musician in genera—he will minor in music in college. He plays extremely well and plays in many different local orchestras and accompanies singers in talent shows—he is really a talent. He not only reads music but can still "just figure it out."

FOOTBALL

I love football, college football in particular. There is nothing like a Saturday of flipping channels and watching parts of as many college games as possible. Justin and I still share long phone calls and emails talking college football—the Georgia Bulldogs and Oklahoma Sooners are our favorite teams. Justin played football from the 5th grade through his junior year in high school. While he may never have had NFL talent, he definitely had the heart to play the game. He absolutely loved the idea of playing a team sport and working with a team to achieve a goal—winning. He was also a pretty good soccer player but once the football bug really bit him he lost interest (it could have been the offensive guard body he had grown into). He played on a couple of really good teams that won many games and championships—the recreation league Wolverines and the

Central Middle School Bandits. However most of the teams he played on including his high school team were average at best in terms of wins and losses but the fun he had and his love of the game were never dampened. We were really involved with his teams with me once calling myself the team doctor—I was the guy that carried the tool box that had the band aides, tape, scissors and a screwdriver in it (figure out later it was to tighten the screws on the helmets). Carol took it a step further and was the lady who ordered and sold the team stuff during the high school games—she had me lugging huge plastic containers with everything from blankets to caps all over the stadium. It was more fun than you could imagine—these were definitely good days!

I'll never forget the day Justin came home from one of his summer practices and proudly told me he was the starting offensive guard on the varsity team. I knew he had gotten to be pretty good, but I was still surprised when he told me the news. What I really appreciated about him was how he really worked hard to earn the position. He was so excited about the upcoming season and believe it or not he was one of those kids who enjoyed the dreaded "two-a-days" even though I doubt he ever told the coaches or his teammates.

The season started and the team while a good team was not a complete team and thus were losing hard fought games. It was fun to watch #52 run out on the field and make his blocks. However I noticed in one game he was not moving as well as he used to but didn't think too much about it since he was still out there. I noticed he came out after halftime wearing a neck collar (a device players wear to help keep their head up while playing).

Later, I asked him about it and he told me he had a "stinger" and had lost the feeling in his arms on one play—this was odd since while I watched the game and the team play I have to be honest my eyes were mostly on #52) and I didn't notice him coming out of the game. I asked him why he didn't just come out of the game. He said the feeling came back after a few plays—I was thinking to myself—he would do anything to stay on the field. Well he was still a little boy at heart and I guess he figured since his legs were working it didn't matter that his arms weren't. Not to make light of the situation but it was amazing how matter-of-fact he was about it all. Like "No big deal Dad—everyone gets a stinger every now and then." Well he got a stinger the next game and we knew it was time to get a doctor to take a look at him. The trip to the doctor turned out to be one of those life-changing events that you remember for the rest of your life. While he and I both thought it would be a routine look and show that he just needed to rest for a while, we were both floored when the doctor came back after reading the x-rays and stated rather bluntly that Justin could never play football or any other contact sport again due to a congenital defect in his neck . I wish I could have said something funny to cheer him up—maybe "now you can take up golf," but the look on his face at that moment was one of pain and disillusionment and this was definitely not a time for humor! I simply grabbed my son and hugged him as tight as I could in an attempt to take all the pain and tears away. As we regained our composure with Carol and the rather callous Doctor looking on (some Doctors really should go through sensitivity training—I don't think this guy had a clue what this meant to my son)—he looked me in the eye and simply said, "guess I'll do something else." How cool was that!! Here he is being told that his football career is over and after a tear or two he is ready to move on! Sure he missed playing football but once he knew he couldn't, it was time to move on. He stayed on the team as the guy who filmed the game for the coaches and did whatever he could to help out. I always knew my knuckleheads would make me proud one day and this was definitely one of those days.

JUSTIN IN CHURCH
(WRITTEN BY JUSTIN GOFF AGE 9)

One Sunday morning I was sitting in church when I started dozing off to sleep. My mom and dad tapped me, but I tried to go to sleep. Then my dad told me to write a story. After a little while church was over and we went to the Fellowship Hall and ate cake and other yummy treats. Then we went home and my dad lectured me about going to sleep in church. Now I won't go to sleep in church anymore. Or will I?

SMOLDERING PAJAMAS ON THE DRIVEWAY

I came home from work one day and as I pulled into the driveway, I noticed what looked like a science experiment gone bad or a piece of clothing smoldering on the driveway. After I pulled into the garage I went out to the driveway to confirm what I hoped was actually a bad science experiment, but sure enough it was a pair of boy pajama pants that had apparently been burning and now were only smoldering. I was surprisingly and almost eerily calm for some reason, I guess I had learned at this point to never be surprised or alarmed by anything that I actually saw my boys doing or thought they might have done. Plus since there were no fire trucks or first responders around and I didn't hear any sirens indicating they were on the way, how bad could it really be!! I go inside and ask no one in particular "Why are there a pair of pajama pants smoldering on the driveway?" Of course there was no initial answer or response since I normally have to repeat what I say at least three times to get a response in my house (usually by yelling the third time). Carol comes out of the bedroom with that "what do you mean pajamas smoldering on the driveway" look on her face. Justin comes out of his room giving his standard answer to any inquiry "I didn't do it" (see item #4 of the boy phrases). Austin of course does not make an appearance at all. He was doing 7 year old boy stuff i.e. laying on his bed twirling his socks. When I asked the no longer presumed but now confirmed guilty party (Austin) what happened, he nonchalantly says "I got my pajama pants wet so I put them on the lights over the sink to dry and they started smoking, so I took them outside and put them on the driveway." His tone was totally matter of fact and his attitude totally nonchalant (like the Cheech and Chong characters) "Like hey man, there was only a little smoke and no fire so "what's the big deal" After his response, Justin, who as the older brother knew what was coming and immediately made like a puff of smoke and vanished, Carol also sensed danger as her motherly instincts to protect her youngest child at all costs kicked in, and she grabbed me right as I was getting ready to pick Austin up and twirl him like he twirled his socks. (Hate to admit it but I even thought about the pajamas smoldering with him in them) Nevertheless, this crisis like all the others passed and as my blood pressure decreased, I calmly had the following exchange with Austin:

ME: Let's not place wet pajamas on the lights over the sink to dry anymore OK Sport

AUSTIN: (sensing now that he may have narrowly avoided a beat down) OK Dad!

IMPLiED TASKS

Our boys are actually five years apart and could not have more different personalities. Even as youngsters it was evident that they were definitely seeing the world out of different colored glasses. The visual Justin and the cerebral Austin, Justin the outgoing life of the party people person and Austin, the not life of the party antisocial person who could literally fade into the woodwork. I would always tell Carol that when they grew up, Justin will probably call us on our birthdays and we might see him for the holidays whereas we would be lucky to hear from Austin every leap year. I had fun over the years noting how different they really were. I am a plant lover and loved to pretend to be a gardener by getting my hands dirty playing in the soil and every so often actually getting a plant to grow. I usually had to drag a long water hose from the outside faucets to my flower beds and various plants I had around the house, It was always a chore lugging the hose all around the house and I couldn't wait for the boys to get old enough to help me by at least rolling the hose back up. One day as I finished watering the plants in the yard, I interrupted Justin as he was watching one of his many favorite cartoons to go out and turn the water off for me. Sure enough he be-bopped out and simply turned the water off and headed back into the house and continued watching his beloved cartoons. Another day, Austin was more of a target of opportunity and I asked him to turn the water off for me as I finished watering the plants. Austin went out and not only turned the water off but rolled up and stored the water hose. I called Justin out again and said "You see how your little brother gets the implied tasks of turning off the water, he not only

turned the water off, but he rolled up and stored the water hose."
Justin looked at me and plainly said, "He's just a suck up and if you
wanted me to roll up the water hose why didn't you just say so!"

So much for implied tasks!

CAMPiNG TRiP

I once took the boys on a camping trip to a lakeside campground in Texas. It was early spring and the weather while a little cool at night was very comfortable during the day. Carol, who considers laying on the deck of a cruise liner "roughing it" in the great outdoors, politely declined our invitation to go with us. "It will be a great time for you and the boys to bond," she said—literal translation NO WAY I'm going to stay in the woods with no bathroom! I left nothing to chance in my preparation for the big camping trip; bedrolls, flashlights, rain gear, matches, snacks, more snacks and I also decided to rent a screened in cabin versus embarrassing myself trying to get the tent set up (this was before the pop up tents and you actually had to put stakes in the ground). While not totally "roughing it," we were still technically sleeping outside plus we had to go to the bathroom outside and the boys thought this was cool. The big day came and me and the boys headed out to the lake side campsite. We got there and immediately starting preparing for the evening by gathering firewood for the campfire. Both of the boys were very excited and while the twigs and blades of grass they brought back would have only generated a spark versus a fire, it was great fun watching my mountain men preparing to live off only what Mother Nature provided. Dinner was actually roasted hot dogs on a skewer, canned pork and beans and smores for dessert. But to them it was wild boar freshly dressed and roasted on a spit over an open fire. We were men of the woods, living off the land and afraid of nothing. Night time came and we were sitting around the fire literally burning smores and I asked the boys if they wanted to hear a campfire story, better yet a scary campfire story. Now better judgment should have kicked in about now but I was caught up in the "mountain men afraid of nothing" routine that I forgot my boys were still very young at the time, and probably didn't know what "scary" really meant. They both loved bedtime stories and often would beg for more from me the "master storyteller"—maybe they just didn't want to go to sleep but I'll go with they loved the way I told and read stories. Tonight though we were going into a new domain—the domain of the scary camp fire story. I decided to tell a story based loosely on an episode of the Twilight Zone that I had watched as a kid. It scared me so bad that I didn't watch Twilight Zone again until I was well into my teens. I didn't even watch Scooby Doo—had too many ghost and zombies. I guess it should have come to mind that my boys were from the same blood line and they probably wouldn't do "scary" too well. But it didn't and I started the story, they were both listening intently as I was really caught up in telling a great story, I suddenly noticed that they both looked horrified and little Austin's eyes were as wide as silver dollars. This was not a look of enjoyment or tell me more Daddy, but it was a look of sheer terror, the "I want my Mommy, let's go home right now" look! I knew then that I had made a huge mistake and quickly tried to phase into a more gentle Disney-esque type story, but the damage was already done! Anything I said after then could well have been from Friday the 13th or some other horror genre movie. I knew I was in for a long night at this point, it was much too late to think about going back home, besides they were frozen with fear and I'm sure they would have broken into a thousand pieces if I had tried to move them. Somehow I managed to convince them to at least get up and go in the cabin, but I knew sleep was out of the question. They wanted so many lights on in the cabin that it was so bright it looked like the sun was inside. I don't think either of them slept more than 10 minutes—I actually think they took turns sleeping to make sure nothing crept in and got them. Morning finally came and our two night camping trip was quickly determined to be only one—we loaded up the truck and headed home. Once we got home, surprisingly the talk was only about building a fire and eating hot dogs and pork and beans out of the can! Not one mention of the scary story Dad told. However, we never went camping again!

FREEZE RAY

My younger brother Bo and I used to play a game we called freeze ray when we were growing up. Back in the day, we took bathtub baths every night versus a shower. My mom always thought we used up more water in the shower (guess an hour shower was too long for her) so we would run a bathtub full of water every night for a bath. Since our house had only one bathroom we obviously had to take turns. There was nothing like relaxing in a hot tub of water and the bathroom lights suddenly go out and a full pitcher of refrigerated ice cold water is dumped on your head and body as you hear "FREEZE RAY." It felt like 1000 volts of electricity, well maybe 10 volts but you get the point, it was a shock! My boys would always get a kick out of me telling the story about Uncle Bo and freeze ray. Bo and I were the youngest and last two at home after our other four siblings had left the nest. I would always tell the boys how much they reminded me of Uncle Bo and I when we were their ages. I guess I should have figured that one day they would want to play some version of the freeze ray game. It happened one day after I had played in a softball tournament where my team played six games before eventually losing in the championship game. I was literally exhausted and couldn't wait to sit in a hot tub of water and relax my aching bones and muscles. I ran the tub of water with anticipation of at least an hour of pure meditation on everything in general and nothing in particular. My body had totally relaxed and I was in the zone of nothingness when the bathroom door suddenly burst open and all I could hear was "FREEZE RAY" as a pitcher of iced water was dumped over my head and body. Fortunately (or maybe unfortunately) most of the water ended up on the bathroom floor but enough got on me to shock me back to my senses. I literally jumped out of the water and could have sworn I saw three shadows quickly exiting the bathroom laughing their little heads off yelling over and over "We gave Daddy the Freeze Ray, We gave Daddy the Freeze Ray". As I stood there naked trying to figure out where I was, I begin thinking, I know it feels like we have more than two boys sometimes but I'm fairly certain there are only two of them. However, I knew I saw three shadows leaving that bathroom. I never really figured it out but I always told myself that it was a young Uncle Bo (who somehow transported himself back to his youth) with the boys that night teaching them the "Freeze Ray" game!

WE'RE GOING TO OKLAHOMA ON A SHIP

We weren't quite sure how we were going to break the news to the Boys about moving to Oklahoma from Florida; we had gone completely "native" in Florida, we didn't even own heavy coats and the boys had never really felt extreme cold weather. But we eventually just sat them down and Carol gave them the "new adventure" story—it always worked on me! Carol came from a military family and moved around all during her childhood and she was very comfortable packing up and moving out. I on the other hand, had rarely traveled more than 150 miles from where I was born and moving was not something I ever got used to even after 20 years in the military. However, the boys seemed to have her vagabond genes when it came to moving and seemed to buy the "new adventure" bit even though Austin was a bit skeptical;

he loved to swim in our backyard pool and kept asking if they had swimming pools in Oklahoma; we assured him there were pools there but never mentioned that he could only swim half of the year versus year round. As a gift for their wonderful attitudes about moving we decided we would take them on a family cruise. We felt they could get their sea legs before we moved to the Midwest and not be able see the ocean as routinely as we did in Florida. We wanted to surprise the boys and didn't tell them right off—we instead told them we were going to Oklahoma for a week to look for a new house. The big day came and we packed up and prepared to head down to the pier in Tampa and the boys still had no clue that we were about to go on their first cruise. We followed our usual long trip routine, packing the night before, checking all of the luggage, making sure they had all of their "are we there yet" avoidance toys and games. We headed out on our journey with a kick of the tires and a full tank of gas and the boys totally oblivious to what was happening. We were running a little late so I headed directly to the pier which took about forty five minutes and as we pulled into the pier parking lot you could see the cruise ship. Justin who by then had probably figured out that we were not driving to Oklahoma looked out the window and saw the cruise ship and said "This is way cool, we gonna go to Oklahoma on a ship!!" Austin who probably didn't know what a cruise ship was, thought this was cool also! We couldn't stop laughing and literally laughed about it all week as we had a wonderful cruise.

While you still can't cruise to Oklahoma on a ship, I have always heard that Oklahoma has more coast line than any other state in the country due to all the man made lakes! Look it up!!

FiRST TiME FiSHiNG

I've loved fishing all of my life and couldn't wait to take the boys on their first fishing trip. While I had some big days on the lake fishing with various fishing buddies, I had also been known to spend a full day on the lake and would literally come home empty handed or "skunked" in fishing vernacular! On these days Carol would meet me at the garage door and cheerily ask "Did you catch anything and I'd go "nope got skunked." While she never said it, I could see that "how can you spend all day fishing and not catch anything" look on her face. Glad she never asked because I would always ask myself the same question and didn't have an answer for me either! Well on the first fishing trip with my boys, I was not too concerned about the boys being afraid of the worms or getting hooked in the ear but my major concern was getting skunked. I thought I played it right when I had a good friend who lived on a lake and would literally feed the fish to bring them to the bank. OK so it wasn't exactly roughing it or fishing for your next meal but it did all but guarantee that we would not be skunked! We got all set up on the fishing dock; rods properly working, right sized hooks on the line, bobbers set at the right depth and worms good and wiggly. Well the plan was working just great, no sooner had we put a line in the water the bobber sunk and Justin pulled up a nice size sunfish— he was sooo excited. Mister "I can do it all by myself" Austin (who insisted on putting the worm on the hook himself) was still trying to figure out exactly how this was supposed to happen. I was hoping he wouldn't just decide to eat the worm—he had been known to sample dog food! In the meantime, Justin's excitement had suddenly turned into a dilemma, I pretended to be helping

Austin and didn't immediately volunteer to take his fish off the hook, I really wanted to see what my little "manly man" would do. The fish was flipping and flopping on the dock and Justin seemed stuck between dropping the rod and running or just throwing the fish back in the water along with the rod and reel! I had my little chuckle and went over to assist and gave him his first "how you take a fish off the hook" lesson. In the middle of this lesson, Austin who had decided not to eat the worm, had finally figured out how to bait his hook and had got his line in the water and like Justin, as soon as the bobber hit the water, it sank as another nice size fish went for the bait. Now I had a dilemma, take the fish off for Justin or help Austin reel in his first fish! Well somehow I did both, I was able to quickly get the hook released from the fish Justin had (he still was not too keen on touching it because it was too slimy) and before Austin's fish could literally pull him in the water, I was able to steady him and get him reeling the fish in! This little circle dance lasted all of 30 seconds and afterward, the boys quickly settled into the routine of bait, cast, and catch fish. We probably caught over thirty fish that day and while we took some home for dinner, most of them we put back into the lake. The fishing trip ended up being a huge success and it was topped off by Austin later innocently asking me "Dad, did I do good at fishing?" I could have melted right then as I answered "Sport you did a great job at fishing."

TOMMY AND DUKE

Neither Carol nor I were big into pets, neither as kids or adults. We did not grow up around pets in our homes and never had any real desire to have them in ours. When Justin was around 4 years old, he pressed for a puppy for a little while after spending the night at a friend's house that had a dog. Once we gave him the facts (what really was intended to be scare tactics) around having a dog i.e. he would have to feed it, walk it, bathe it and take it out to do it's "business," he quickly backed off and went off to play with his Teenage Mutant Ninja Turtles. We felt great and assumed we had put the pet talk to rest. Well Austin was a little more persistent and once he realized that a puppy was out of the question he tried another angle. He tried the old, "if I can't have a dog what other pet can I have" routine on us! As I quickly ruled out "all pets" he was persistent in reading his list of the types of pets that existed other than dogs! He rightfully assumed that if a dog was out, a cat should not be on the pet consideration list either. He started with the classroom friendly and low maintenance gerbil—nice try! Then the guinea pig—forget it, it's still essentially a rat! His aunt used to have a parrot that actually talked but I think even Austin was a little afraid of that parrot! He finally landed on gold fish which even to me seemed like a risk free and low maintenance proposition, just a fish bowl and two fish—how hard could it be! We immediately went out and bought a fish bowl, and I do mean a fish bowl, not a fancy aquarium with a little lost treasure on the bottom but a bowl that we simply added water and put the fish in! Since it was Austin's idea, not only did he get the fish bowl in his bedroom, but he also got to name the fish. He named them Tommy and Duke after two characters from a kid show he watched. For the first few days, Tommy and Duke seemed to be two of the happiest gold fish on earth; they swam happily and ate their fill. Now I didn't recall much of what the pet store guy said but I did remember him saying something like the fish should only be fed once a day with maybe two shakes of the fish food. Well to a 4 year old, two shakes of anything is not enough and once a day means the fish would obviously starve!! While I didn't see him do it, I am sure Austin fed those fish every time he looked up and saw them in the fish bowl. After awhile the novelty of the fish in the fish bowl began to wear off, Tommy and Duke were left under the caring watch of Austin and the rest of us were content with this arrangement. However about a week later there was a noticeable smell coming out of Austin's room and I went in and saw that the fish bowl was a murky mess of fish food and two dead fish. Tommy and Duke had literally exploded from what I assumed was eating too much—they ate themselves to death! Austin apparently had forgotten about the two shakes of fish food and went to the "dump as much food as possible" mode of feeding Tommy and Duke! We quickly made funeral arrangements for Tommy and Duke (fishing net to the toilet) and gave them a royal flush service—flushed them down the toilet! The fish bowl was emptied and tossed out, the bedroom was fumigated and all was back to normal in the Goff house. No pets allowed!

It should be noted that Austin never gave up on his dream of having a pet—when he was 13, we moved to New York and one of his request to help him adjust to the move was to get a puppy. This is where Rusty the Pug came into our lives but this is another story to be told at another time.

JUST WATCH ME

A promotion ceremony is one of many proud traditions of the United States Military. Carol and I were blessed to have eight (four each) such ceremonies over the course of our twenty year careers in the United States Air Force. Not only were we fortunate enough to have earned promotions but we were even more fortunate to "pin on" our new ranks usually around the same time. One of our most memorable promotion ceremonies was our last one. We were both being promoted to the rank of Lieutenant Colonel and had invited all of our family members, friends and fellow military members to attend our ceremony at MacDill Air Force Base in Tampa, Florida. It was an exciting event that we planned very carefully, since I was fairly certain it would be my last promotion before retirement. Carol was still thinking she was going to serve longer (we both officially retired 3 years later) thus she didn't feel or have the same sense of finality that I felt. During the ceremony the new romote gets an opportunity to address the audience and it is usually a time to thank their mentors and those who had a hand in helping them get promoted. I used this opportunity to publicly talk to Justin and Austin and give them what I hoped would be one of the most valuable gifts they could ever get from me—being their role model!! I titled my address "Just Watch Me" and the following is an excerpt from the speech:

I would like to thank all of you who have come today to honor us with your presence for our promotion ceremony. I would like to take a few moments to thank a few special people in the audience. First of all, thank you Gen Noonan for presiding over my part of the ceremony—it has been a real blast to work for and serve with you. Thanks to Col Wahlquist for his support and advice and many thanks to all of my co-workers, both civilian and military. My heartfelt thanks to my family especially my (Mother and Father) and dear friends who have traveled long distances to be here today. But I reserve the most special thanks to my wife, Carol—Mrs. Lt Col Goff and my two knuckleheads (my sons Justin and Austin) The next few minutes and words are really geared toward them (pointing at my knuckleheads). Today before this gathering I promise to you that you will never have to look to some famous athlete or movie star to be your role model, to be someone to show and teach you how to be the man you should be and a productive citizen in our society. JUST WATCH ME! That's my job as your FATHER and I eagerly and readily accept the responsibility to tell you and more importantly show you how to take initiative and accept responsibility for your actions, how to be compassionate yet stern in your beliefs, how to love hard, how to be a loyal and faithful friend, how to be willing to take action when all others are watching, how to act like and be a good man!! Just watch your father, I will show you the way—I will be your Role Model!!! Boys (JUST WATCH ME)—I accept that responsibility as you Father!

Thanks and Bless you all for being here today!

EXCERPTS FROM CHRISTMAS LETTERS PAST

I'm not totally sure how the Christmas Letter craze started and don't really know if I want to curse or kiss whoever started it, but we have been doing them for over 20 years. Since I am the designated "Author" in my house, I have the responsibility to make sure the letter is written in enough time to get stuffed and mailed in the Christmas Cards, in our case usually two days before Christmas. I would always sarcastically tell Carol that I thought the idea was for our friends to get the Christmas cards *before* Christmas, she would then give me that same Medusa like stare that her Mother would give me when I said something she deemed stupid! Thus the Christmas Cards were sent out two days before Christmas and I was OK with that.

It seemed odd that I had the task of writing the Christmas letter since it was usually an update on what was happening with the family and I was probably the least informed on what was happening in our household. However, over the years it became one of my more memorable and enjoyable "chores." Like most Christmas letters ours centered around the growth and shenanigans of our boys, how much they had grown, how well they were doing in school, how many instruments they were playing and just generally the good stuff. Like our friends I would go on and on about how the boys were doing and how proud they were making us because after all it was Christmas and why ruin the holidays talking about the house almost being burned down by wet pajamas being place on the light fixtures in the bathroom! Christmas is a happy time and we always wanted our friends to think happy thoughts when they thought of us raising our two boys!

The following are a few excerpts from Christmas Letters past: (You should note many of the chapter titles for this book come from these Letters)

Christmas Letter 2003

As usual our two knuckleheads, Justin and Austin, have been the focus of our lives. They are both big boys now, but they are still Mama's babies—I will be glad when they get their own wives, so I can stop asking *When Do I Get my Wife Back*!!!!

Justin, who has changed his name to J-Dizzle, is now 16 and is a fairly typical teenager. J-Dizzle (who often refers to himself in the third person—"J-Dizzle is hungry"), plays bass guitar in a band called PUSHOVER (while they may not be Grammy material yet, they can play!). J-Dizzle also lettered in varsity football (offensive and defensive line). The team had 1 win and 9 losses for the year, but according to J-Dizzle they will be much better next year. J-Dizzle also watches too much TV, picks on his little brother and eats ALL the time. J-Dizzle really keeps us entertained and while we will miss him, we are looking forward to the day when Justin returns.

Austin is now 11, and continues to grow both physically and mentally. He will soon make Carol the shortest person in our house. He continues to excel in school and is still on track to change the world as we know it! Our attempt to round him off by making him participate in athletics has been somewhat successful—he likes golf and gymnastics. In gymnastics, he has advanced to a higher class of competition, and still amazes us with all of the things he can do with his body. He started playing piano by ear on his own (according to him "*I Just Figured It Out*"). He is now taking piano lessons and he seems to enjoy it for now!

Christmas Letter 2005

Justin is now 18 and almost Ready For The World. He will graduate in the spring and hopefully attend a fine institution of higher learning (Georgia, Oklahoma or any school that will take him). We survived the Afro, J-Dizzle (his alter ego from a few years back), Pushover (his punk rock band), two totally wrecked cars (Mercedes and Jeep), and the messiest bedroom this side of the Mississippi. But at the end of the day we wouldn't have had it any other way—well actually we could have done without the wrecked cars (smile). No book can teach you how to raise kids, especially boys, so you just work and pray your way through it. We are extremely proud of Justin and know we are sending a fine young man out to make his mark on the world. Send money for his graduation—he needs a vehicle (smile).

Not only are we losing Justin, but we have also lost Austin to the dreaded TEENAGE YEARS! He turned 13 in November and while it has been calm so far, we are keeping a close eye on him—we know the pod will open soon. He has become a pretty good musician—first chair Viola in the school orchestra and has nimble fingers on the piano. It's interesting in the mornings to hear classical piano coming out of Austin's room and loud whatever you call it, coming out of Justin's room. While they are still pretty much knuckleheads, we are very proud of them both.

WHY THiS BOOK

I have threatened my wife and boys with writing this book for years and while the story line is still ongoing, I feel it was time to get it out of the computer and out for public consumption. I love my boys (who are now Men) very much but I am especially happy about the time we spent together while they were "little fellas" seeing the wonders of the world for the first time. If I have any regret, it is that the time was too short and they literally (and figuratively) grew up too fast. I hope and pray that they too get to experience the world again and for the first time through their own kids eyes as I have through theirs and more than anything else, I hope they continue to see *King Kong Ridin' on a Half a Hot Dog*!

Edwards Brothers Malloy
Thorofare, NJ USA
January 10, 2017